ORCHIDS

ORCHIDS

PETER MURRAY

THE CHILD'S WORLD®

Walking through the Brazilian rainforest, you see plenty of leaves and vines and tree trunks. A colorful parrot might catch your eye, but mostly what you see is a tangle of green and brown and black and gray.

Suddenly, a splash of brilliant color appears against the jungle green. High on the trunk of a tall tree, shining like a bright pink star, you see your first wild orchid.

It looks like something from another planet, or like a flower in a dream. You take its picture, but leave the plant alone.

At the same time, five thousand miles away, a girl is going to her high school prom. Her date arrives at the door and hands her a box. Inside the box, she finds a beautiful corsage: a small bouquet of flowers for her to pin on her dress. In the center of the corsage is a large, bright pink orchid.

The orchid in the girl's corsage bloomed in a greenhouse, but it is a close relative of the wild rainforest orchid. They are both members of the *Cattleya* genus, one of the most beautiful and widely grown orchids.

The orchid family is the largest in the plant kingdom. Scientists have discovered and named more than 25,000 species of wild orchids. Some orchids have blossoms no larger than the head of a nail. Others have flowers the size of a dinner plate—much too big to pin on a dress! Wild orchids live on every continent. They grow in nearly every environment from frozen Arctic tundra to steamy African rainforests. The only place you won't find an orchid is in very dry environments like deserts.

Many tropical orchids are *epiphytes*. Epiphytes grow high in the treetops, clinging by their roots to tree branches. Their roots draw moisture from the surrounding air and from rain that runs down the tree trunks. Other orchid species are *terrestrial*, meaning that they grow in the soil like most other plants. The *showy lady's slipper* prefers the cool, boggy soils of the north woods. Some Australian species actually grow underground. These plants peek through the dirt only when they are ready to bloom. Orchids native to the Arctic push up through the melting spring snow to bloom.

When people brought tropical orchids to Europe in the 1700s, they tried to grow them in hot, dry greenhouses. The orchid plants withered and died without flowering. By the early 1800s, a few growers had learned that tropical orchids need plenty of fresh air, humidity, and cool nights. The growers who successfully produced orchid blossoms kept their methods secret. Because orchids were so rare and difficult to obtain, they became very valuable, sometimes selling for hundreds of dollars each.

All orchid blossoms share the same basic structure. There are three *petals*—two petals on top, and one specially shaped petal, called the *lip,* on the bottom. Behind the petals are three *sepals.* On most flowers, the sepals are small and green. Orchid sepals can be almost any color, and sometimes they are larger than the petals.

The oddly shaped lower petal is different for every species of orchid. Cattleya orchids have a ruffled, trumpet-shaped lip. Lady's slipper orchids have a pouch-shaped lip that looks like a slipper. Some orchids, like this one, are almost impossible to describe!

Wild orchids *pollinate* one another by using their blossoms to attract insects. The *Trichoceros* orchid has a lip petal that looks like a fly. The male fly is fooled into thinking the petal is a female fly! When the fly lands, the orchid's pollen sticks him. When he visits another orchid plant, pollen rubs off him and onto the flower's *stigma*. This pollinates the plant, allowing seeds to form.

The lady's slipper uses scent to attract its pollinator. A hungry insect visits the plant expecting to find sweet nectar, but it is trapped inside the slipper. The insect quickly escapes—but it is covered with pollen!

Orchid seeds are so small you could hold millions of them in your hand. For many years, orchid growers could not figure out how to grow orchids from seed. The mystery was solved in the mid-1800s, when it was discovered that soil had to contain a certain type of fungus for the seeds to sprout.

Once they learned how to grow orchids from seeds, growers were able to create *hybrids*. Hybrids are formed when the pollen from one orchid fertilizes the seeds of a different species of orchid, creating an entirely new variety. Orchid growers have now created more than 75,000 hybrids.

Most orchids are grown for their beauty, but one species is grown for another reason. Every time you eat a bowl of ice cream or a vanilla wafer, you are enjoying the flavor of the *vanilla* orchid. Long before Europeans discovered America, the Aztecs were using the long brown seed pods of the vanilla orchid for flavoring.

The vanilla orchid is a climbing, vinelike plant with large yellow flowers. Today, the vanilla orchid is nearly extinct in the wild because its forest habitat is being destroyed to make room for farms and cities. Most vanilla plants now grow on huge farms on Madagascar, off the coast of Africa.

Orchids are very sensitive to their environment. They need the right amount of sunlight, moisture, and soil, and the soil must contain the special fungi that help the seeds develop. Each orchid species relies on a particular insect species for pollination. If any one of these needs is missing, the orchid will not thrive. Many orchid species are already extinct or endangered because their habitat has been disturbed or destroyed.

We can breed thousands of hybrid orchid varieties, but we cannot replace millions of years of evolution. Once a wild species is gone, it is gone forever.

INDEX

Photo Research

Kristee Flynn

Photo Credits

Robert & Linda Mitchell: cover, 7, 13, 14, 21, 24, 31

Tony Arruza: 2

BRUCE COLEMAN INC. / Erwin & Peggy Bauer: 4

PHOTO RESEARCHERS, INC. / Robert Bornemann: 8

BRUCE COLEMAN INC. / Carlos V. Causo: 11

Kevin Schafer: 17

Ron Kimball: 18

BRUCE COLEMAN INC. / Andrew Rackoczy: 22

Peter Arnold, Inc. / Roland Seitre: 27

PHOTO RESEARCHERS, INC. / Karl Weidmann: 28

Library of Congress Cataloging-in-Publication Data
Murray, Peter, 1952 Sept. 29-
Orchids / by Peter Murray.
p. cm.
Includes Index.
ISBN 1-56766-194-7

1. Orchids--Juvenile literature.   [1. Orchids.]   I. Title.
QK495.064M87   1995   95-906
584'.15--dc20